A Profit Manual for REALTORS®

How to Attract More Real Estate Clients

by Vincent Davis

COPYRIGHT AND DISCLAIMER

This material is copyright. No part, in whole or in part, may be reproduced by any process, or any other exclusive right exercised, without the permission of www.legalmarketingandsalescoach.com

© 2017 Vincent Davis

VINCENT DAVIS

Published by:
Leader Publishing Worldwide
19 Axford Bay
Port Moody, BC V3H 3R4
Tel: 1 888-297-1616

Fax: 1 877 575 9151
Website: www.EliteMarketingAndSalesCoach.com

ISBN-13: 978-1718933972
ISBN-10: 1718933975

DISCLAIMER AND/OR LEGAL NOTICES:
While every attempt has been made to verify information provided in this book, neither the author nor the publisher assumes any responsibility for any errors, omissions or inaccuracies.

Any slights of people or organizations are unintentional. If advice concerning legal or related matters is needed, the services of a qualified professional should be sought. This book is not intended as a source of legal or accounting advice. You should be aware of any laws which govern business transactions or other business practices in your state or province.

The income statements and examples are not intended to represent or guarantee that everyone will achieve the same results. Each individual's success will be determined by his or her desire, dedication, effort, and motivation. There are no guarantees you will duplicate the results stated here, you recognize that any business endeavor has inherent risk for loss of capital.

Any reference to any persons or business, whether living or deceased, existing or defunct, is purely coincidental.

PRINTED IN THE USA

DEDICATION

I would like to dedicate this book to my only son, Vinny, who lost his battle with drug addiction. Son, I may have never told you this but you, and your sister, were and are the loves of my life. I have taken many things we discussed and put into this book. I hope to make you proud.

CONTENTS

1 Create a Powerful Offer 5
2 Use Scripts to Get Listings and Buyers Fast 11
3 Immediate Clients 23
4 Double Your Referrals 35
5 Profit Over the Phone 45
6 Generate Unlimited Leads 61
7 Profits and Leads through Host-Beneficiary Relationships 73
8 Use Press Releases for Instant Profit 87
9 Profit from Direct Mail 109
10 Organize Your Office for Success 115
So What Do You Do From Here? 123

INTRODUCTION

This is the first page, but by opening this book you have already taken an important step towards increasing the success of your real estate business. Congratulations in your quest to enhance your marketing skills

When I put pen to paper I found myself with an enormous amount of information I've developed over a 30 year career as an attorney, and with my own practice for 27 years. Many marketing experts have not built their own businesses. I, on the other hand, have been sitting across the desk from potential clients for more than 30 years; and I've run my own firm for the past 30 years. And as of this writing, my firm is still running with 12 full time associates. The principles I've learned over the years can be valuable to any real estate professional as well.

The strategies and techniques in this book have been developed over 30 years in the trenches, and literally with hundreds and hundreds of clients. The strategies in this book, when implemented with consistency and care, are guaranteed to make you more money with less effort. These are strategies have helped businesspeople make hundreds of thousands of dollars, including your competitors.

This is the reason I have dedicated my life to marketing and business consulting. Since starting my marketing company, I want to provide direction for small and medium real estate businesses. I have been literally overwhelmed with the demand for marketing and business consulting.

A Profit Manual for Realtors®

As you follow the book and read the principles, remember it does not matter what type of type of business you are in. What matters is that your grasp the heart of the principles, the underlying lessons and strategies, that can help grow your real estate business.

The best time to start is now, not tomorrow, not next week or next year.

Yours in success,

Vince Davis
Attorney at Law

P. S. If you would like to arrange a meeting to get a profitable third party perspective on your business, please send an email to v@elitemarketingandsalescoach.com and we will gladly point you in the right direction.

To learn how to avoid the three key mistakes all small and medium firms make, visit www.EliteMarketingAndSalesCoach.com

1

Create a Powerful Offer

I'm not going to beat around the bush on this one:

Your offer is the granite foundation of your marketing campaign.

Get it right, and everything else will fall into place. Your headline will grab readers, your copy will sing, your ad layout will hardly matter, and you will have clients running to your door.

Get it wrong, and even the best looking, best-written campaign will sink like the Titanic.

A powerful offer is an irresistible offer. It's an offer that gets your audience frothing at the mouth and clamoring over each other all the way to your door. An offer that makes your readers pick up the phone to do business with you as their Realtor®.

Irresistible offers make your potential clients think, "I'd be crazy not to take him up on that," or "An offer like this doesn't come around very often." They instill a sense of emotion, of desire, and ultimately, urgency.

Make it easy for clients to list or purchase a property from you the first time, and they'll call you first when it comes time to buy or sell.

I'll say it again: **get it right, and everything else will fall into place.**

The Crux of Your Marketing Campaign

As you work your way through this program, you will find that nearly every chapter discusses the importance of a powerful offer as related to your marketing strategy or promotional campaign.

There's a reason for this. The powerful offer is more often than not the reason a client will open their wallets. It is how you generate leads, and then convert them into loyal clients. The more dramatic, unbelievable, and valuable the offer is the more dramatic and unbelievable the response will be.

Many companies spend thousands of dollars on impressive marketing campaigns in glossy magazines and big city newspapers. They send massive direct mail campaigns on a regular basis; yet don't receive an impressive or massive response rate.

These companies do not yet understand that simply providing information on their company and the benefits of their product is not enough to get clients to act. There is no reason to pick up the phone *right now*.

Your powerful, irresistible offer can:
- Increase leads
- Drive traffic to your website or business
- Convert leads into clients
- Build your prospective client database

What Makes a Powerful Offer?

A powerful offer is one that makes the most people respond, and take action. It gets people running to spend money on your product or service.

Powerful offers nearly always have an element of *urgency* and of *scarcity*. They give your audience a reason to act immediately, instead of put it off until a later date.

Urgency relates to time. The offer is only available until a certain date, during a certain period of the day, or if you act within a few hours of seeing the ad. The client needs to act now to take advantage of the offer.

Scarcity related to quantity. There are only a certain number of clients who will be able to take advantage of the offer. There may be a limited number of spaces, a limited number of products, or simply a limited number of people the business will provide the offer to. Again, this requires that client acts immediately to reap the high value for low cost.

Powerful offers also:

Offer great value. Clients perceive the offer as having great value – more than the average Realtor® can offer. It could be your proven system to help sellers get more money for their houses faster. It could be your huge database of prospective buyers. It could be extra services you offer to help a buyer find their dream home or investment property. It is clear that the offer takes the reader's needs and wants into consideration.

Make sense to the reader. They are simple and easy to understand if read quickly. There are no "catches" or requirements;

no fine print.

Seem logical. The offer doesn't come out of thin air. There is a logical reason behind it – a holiday, end of season, anniversary celebration, or new listing. People can get suspicious of offers that seem "too good to be true" and have no apparent purpose.

Provide a premium. The offer provides something extra to the client, like a free gift, or free product or service. They feel they are getting something extra for no extra cost. Premiums are perceived to have more value than discounts.

Remember that when your target market reads your offer, they will be asking the following questions:

1. What will you do for me if I buy or list with you?
2. What's in it for me?
3. What makes me sure I can believe you?

The Most Powerful Types of Offers

Decide what kind of offer will most effectively achieve your objectives. Are you trying to generate leads, convert clients, build a database, or generate referrals?

Consider what type of offer will be of most value to your ideal clients – what offer will make them act quickly.

Free Offer

This type of offer asks clients to act immediately in exchange for something free. This is a good strategy to use to build a client database or mailing list. Offer a free consultation, free consumer report, free book on buying or selling real estate or other

Create a Powerful Offer

item of low cost to you but of high perceived value.

You can also advertise the value of the item you are offering for free. For example, act now and you'll receive a free book, worth $19.95. This will dramatically increase your lead generation, and allow you to focus on conversion when the client comes through the door or picks up the phone.

The Value Added Offer

Add additional services or products that cost you very little, and combine them with other items to increase their attractiveness. This increases the perception of value in the client's mind, which will justify increasing the price of a product or service without incurring extra hard costs to your business. How can you provide more value to a buyer or seller than the average Realtor® can?

Urgency Offer

As I mentioned above, offers that include an element of urgency enjoy a better response rate, as there is a reason for your clients to act immediately. Give the offer a deadline or limit the number of spots available.

Guarantee Offer

Offer to take the risk of making a purchase away from your clients. Guarantee the performance or results of your service, and offer to compensate the client if you can't deliver. One successful California broker advertises that he will buy your house if he can't find a buyer with a reasonable offer in a given period of time. Of course you really need to know what you are doing to pull this off. This will help overcome any fear or reservations about your service, and make it more likely for your leads to become clients.

Create Your Powerful Offer

1. Decide what you want your clients to do.

What are you looking to achieve from your offer? If it is to generate more leads, then you'll need your client to contact you. Do you want them to visit your website? Sign up for your newsletter? How long do they have to act? Be clear about your call to action, and state it clearly in your offer.

2. Dream up the biggest, best offer.

First, think of the biggest, best things you could offer your clients – regardless of cost and ability. Don't limit yourself to a single type of offer, combine several types of offers to increase value. Offer a premium, plus a guarantee, with a package offer. Then take a look at what you've created, and make the necessary changes so it is realistic.

3. Run the numbers.

Finally, make sure the offer will leave you with enough profit to make it worthwhile. You don't want to publish an outrageous offer that will generate a tremendous number of leads, but leave you busy doing tasks that don't result in listings and buyers. Remember that each client has an acquisition cost, as well as a immediate and potential lifetime value.

2

Use Scripts to Get Listings and Buyers Fast

What do playbooks, prompts, guides and scripts all have in common?

They are all popular tools that dictate or guide human behavior toward a desired outcome.

Playbooks help coaches tell sports teams specifically how to play the game to overcome an opponent. Prompts help to kick-start writers and other creative professionals when stuck in a rut. Guides provide a series of instructions so that a person or team of people can complete or implement a specific task. Film scripts tell actors how to act for a particular part.

If you're in the business of sales, you also know about sales scripts. Sales scripts are tools that guide salespeople during interactions or conversations with potential clients.

A large number of businesses use scripts, either as a way of maintaining consistency amongst a sales team, training new salespeople, or enhancing their sales skills. They may have a single script, or several, and may change their scripts regularly, or use the same one for years.

What most businesses overlook, however, is that the sales script is a living, breathing, changing member of their sales team. They may be internal documents, but they deserve just as much time and effort as your marketing collateral.

Do You Really Need a Script?

The short answer is yes. You absolutely need a script for any and every client interaction you and your salespeople may find yourselves in.

Sure, countless brokers and Realtors® work every day without a script. If you own your own business, chances are you're already a pretty good salesperson. But if you are not using scripts, you're only working at half of your true potential – or half of your potential earnings.

Scripts don't have to be "cheesy" or read verbatim. They act as a map for your sales process, and provide prompts to trigger your memory and keep you on track. How many times have you talked with a prospect, and it didn't work out the way you wanted it to? Scripts dramatically improve the effectiveness and efficiency of your sales processes.

A comprehensive set of scripts will also keep a level of consistency amongst your salespeople and the client service they provide your clients.

Once scripts are written, memorized, and rehearsed, they become like film scripts; the salesperson can breathe their own life and personality into the conversation, while staying focused on the call's objectives.

Why Your Scripts Aren't Working

If you a currently using scripts in your business, are they working? Are they as effective as they could possibly be? How do you know? When was the last time they were reviewed or updated?

Scripts are like any other element of your marketing campaign – they need to be tested and measured for results, and changed based on what is or is not working.

Measure the success of your script based on your conversion rates. Of all the people you speak to and use the script, how many are being converted from leads to listings or sales?

When evaluating your existing scripts, ask yourself the following questions:

How old is this script? What was it written for? Scripts are living, breathing members of your company. They need to be written and rewritten and rewritten again as the needs of your clients change, as the market changes, or as new strategies are implemented.

Does this script address all the client objections we regularly hear? Every time you hear a client raise an objection that is not included on the script, add it. The power of your script lies in the ability to anticipate client concerns, and answer them before they're raised.

Does this script sound the same as the others? Your scripts are part of the package that represents you as a professional. There should be a consistent feel or approach throughout your scripts that your clients will recognize and feel confident dealing with.

Is everyone using the script? Who on your team regularly uses these scripts? Just the junior staff? Only the top-performing staff? Make sure everyone is singing from the same song sheet – your clients will appreciate the consistency.

Types of Scripts

Depending on the types of real estate you sell and the marketing strategies you have chosen, there are countless types of scripts you could potentially prepare for your business,

When you sit down to create your scripts, it would be wise to start by making a list of all the instances you and your staff members interact with your existing or potential clients. Then, prioritize the list from most to least important, and start writing from the top.

Here are some commonly used scripts, and their purposes:

Listing Acquisition script

Each time you or your agents make a presentation, they should be using the same or a slightly modified version of the same script. This script will include sample icebreakers, a presentation on benefits and features of listing or buying with your company, and a list of possible objections and responses. These scripts should also help alleviate some of the nervousness or anxiety associated with public speaking.

Closing script

Closing scripts help you do just that: close the sale. This could include a list of closing prompts or statements to get the transaction started. This type of script also includes a list of possible client objections, and planned responses.

Use Scripts to Get Listings and Buyers Fast

Incoming phone call script

Everyone who calls your company should be treated the same way; consistent information should be gathered and provided to the client. The person answering the phone should state the company name, department name, and their own name in the initial greeting. This goes for both the main line, and each individual or department extension.

Cold call script

This is one of the most important scripts you can perfect for your business. The cold call script must master the art of quickly getting the attention of the client, then engaging and persuading them with the benefits of working with you. The caller needs to establish common ground with the potential client, and find a way to get them talking through open-ended questions.

Direct mail follow-up script

Scripts for outgoing calls that are intended to follow up on a direct mail piece are essential for every direct mail campaign. They are designed to call qualified leads that have already received information, and convert them into clients. These scripts should focus on enticing clients to act, and overcoming any objections that may have prevented them from acting sooner.

Market research script

Scripts that are used primarily for the purpose of gathering information should be designed to get the client talking. A focus on open-ended questions and relationship building statements will help to relax the client, and encourage honest dialogue.

A Profit Manual for Realtors®

Difficult client script

Just like every salesperson needs to practice the sales process, you and your staff also need to practice your ability to handle difficult clients. These scripts should help you diffuse the situation, calm the client down, and then handle their objections.

Creating Scripts

Creating powerful scripts is not a complicated exercise, but it will take some time to complete. Focus on the most vital scripts for your business first, and engage the assistance of your sales staff in drafting or reviewing the scripts.

Your Script Binder

Keep master copies of all of your scripts in one organized place. An effective way to do this is to create a binder, and use tabs to separate each type of script.

You will also want to create a separate tab for client objections, and list every single client objection you have ever heard in relation to your service. Find a way to organize each objection so you can easily find them – group them by category or separate them with tabs.

Then, list your responses next to each objection – there should be several responses to each objection created with different client types in mind. A master list of client objections and responses is an invaluable tool for any business owner, salesperson, and script writer. The more responses you can think of, the better.

Use Scripts to Get Listings and Buyers Fast

Remember, the script binder is never "finished." You will need to make sure that it is updated and added to on a regular basis.

Writing Scripts – Step by Step

Step One: Record What You're Doing Now

If you aren't using scripts – or even if you are – start by recording yourself in action. Use video or audio recording to tape yourself on the phone, in a sales presentation, or with a client.

Make notes on your body language, word choice, client reaction and body language, responses to objections, and closing statements.

You may also wish to ask an associate to make notes on your performance and discuss them with you in a constructive fashion.

Step Two: Evaluate What You're Doing Wrong

Take a look at your notes, and ask yourself the following questions:

- How are you engaging the client?
- Are you building common ground and trust?
- Does what you are saying matter to the client?
- Is your offer a powerful one?
- What objections are raised?
- How are you dealing with them?
- What objections are you avoiding?
- How natural is your close?
- Are you as effective as you think you can be?

Once you have answered and made notes in response to these questions, make a list of things you need to improve, and how you think you might go about doing so. Do you need to strengthen your closing statements? Do you need to brainstorm more responses to objections? Remember that everyone's script and sales process can be improved.

Step Three: Decide Who the Script is For

So now that you know the elements of your script you need to work on, you can begin drafting your new script, or revising an old one.

The first part of writing a script – or any piece of marketing material – is having a strong understanding of who you are writing it for. Who is your target audience? What does your ideal client look like? Consider demographic characteristics like age, sex, location, income, occupation and marital status. Be as specific as possible.

If you are writing a cold call script, you will need to develop or purchase a list of people who fall into the target market specifics you have established. Spend some time reviewing what types of clients are in the market for the properties you normally sell.

You will want to use words that your target audience will not only understand, but relate to and resonate with. Use sensory language that will trigger emotional and feeling responses – *I need this, this will solve that problem, I'll feel better if I use this Realtor®, etc.*

Step Four: Decide What You Want to Say

There are typically five sections of every script – and there may be more, depending on the type and purpose of script:

1. Engage

- Get their attention or pique their interest
- Establish common ground

Use Scripts to Get Listings and Buyers Fast

- Build trust, be human
- Ask for their time

2. Ask + Qualify

- Take control of the conversation by asking questions
- Focus on open-ended questions that cannot be answered with a "yes" or "no"
- Get the client talking
- Ask as many questions as you need to get information on the client's needs and purchase motivations

3. Get Agreement

- Ask closed-ended questions you are sure they will respond with "yes"
- Get them to agree on the benefits of the product or service
- Repeat key points back to the client to gain agreement

4. Overcome Objections

- Anticipate objections based on client comments, then refute them
- Make informative assumptions about their thought process, identify with their concern, then refute it using your own experiences
- Repeat concerns back to the client to let them know you have heard them
- Ask about any remaining objections before you close

5. Close

- Assume that you have overcome all objections, and have the sale

- Ask the client transactional questions, like delivery timing and payment method
- Be as confident and natural as possible

Step Five: Train Your Staff

Once you have written your company's scripts, you will need to ensure your staff understand and are comfortable using them.

Consider having a team meeting, and use role play to review each of the scripts. This will encourage your agents to practice amongst each other, and strengthen their sales skills. Ask them for feedback on the scripts, and make any necessary changes.

You will also need to decide how comfortable you are having your agents personalizing the scripts to suit their own styles. Be clear what elements of the script are "company standards" and essential techniques, but also be flexible with your team.

Step Six: Continually Revise

After you have carefully crafted your script, put it to the test. Practice on your colleagues, friends, and family. Get their feedback, and make changes.

Remember that scripts will need to change and evolve as your business changes and evolves, and new products or services are introduced. Keep your script binder on your desk at all times, and continually make changes and improvements to it.

You may also wish to record and evaluate your performance on a regular basis. This is an exercise you could incorporate into regular employee reviews, to use as a constructive tool for staff development.

Use Scripts to Get Listings and Buyers Fast

Script Tips

- Practice anticipating and eliciting real objections – including the ones your client doesn't want to raise.
- Make the script yours – it should look, feel, and sound like you naturally do, not like you're reading off the page.
- Spend time with the masters. If there is a salesperson you admire in your community, ask to observe them in action. Take notes on their performance, and the techniques they use for success.
- If your script is not successful, ask the client why not? Even if you don't get the sale, you'll get a new objection you can craft responses to and never get stumped by it again.
- Don't fear objections. Just spend time identifying as many as possible, then practice overcoming them.
- Never stop thinking of responses to client objections. Each objection could potentially have 30 responses, geared toward specific client types.
- Anecdotes are persuasive writing tools – use them in your scripts. People enjoy hearing stories, especially stories that relate to them and their experiences, frustrations, and troubles. Let the story sell your product or service for you.
- Include body language in your scripts – it's just as important as your words. Try mimicking your subject's posture, arm position, and seating position. This is proven to create ease and build trust.
- If you only have your voice, use it. Pay attention to tone, language choice, speed, and background noise. You only have sound to establish a trusting relationships, so do it carefully.
- Be confident, and focus on a positive stream of self-talk to prepare for the call or presentation. Confidence sells.

A Profit Manual for Realtors®

Spend time on your closing scripts, as they are a critical component of your presentation or phone call. This can be a challenging part of the sales process, so practice, practice, practice.

3

Immediate Clients

If you're a broker, you've had to sell the bank to get them to loan you your start-up capital. You've had to convince your business partner, spouse, and friends why your business idea is a good one. And you have to sell yourself as the client's best choice to help them buy or sell their property.

The ability to sell effectively and efficiently is one every successful business owner has cultivated, and continues to develop. It can be a complicated and time consuming task; one that you will have to continually work on throughout your career in order to be – and stay – successful.

Fortunately, making sales is a step-by-step process that can be learned, customized, and continuously improved. There are a wide range of tools available to help and support your sales efforts.

You don't have to be the most outgoing, enthusiastic person to be successful at sales. You don't even have to be a good public speaker. All you need is an understanding of the basic sales process, and a genuine passion for what you are selling.

Sales 101

As I said before, making sales is a process. There are clear, step-by-step actions that can be taken and result in a sale.

The sales process varies according to the type of property and the type of client you are working with; however, the core steps are the same. Similarly, sales training varies from individual to individual, but the core skills and abilities remain the same.

Here is a basic seven-step process that you can follow, or fine tune to suit your unique properties and services. Remember that each step is important, and builds on the step previous. It is essential to become adept at each step, instead of solely focusing on closing the sale.

1. Preparation

Make sure you have prepared for your meeting, presentation. You have complete control of this part of the sales process, so it is important to do everything you can to set the stage for your success.

- Understand the sales and listing process inside and out.
- Prepare all the necessary materials, and organize them neatly.
- Keep your place of business tidy and organized.
- Ensure you appear professional and well groomed.
- Do some research on your potential client and brainstorm to find common ground.

2. Build a Relationship

The first few minutes you spend with a potential client set the stage for the rest of your interaction. First impressions are everything. Your goal in the second step is to relax the client and

Immediate Clients

begin to develop a relationship with them. Establishing a real relationship with your client will create trust.

- Make a great first impression: shake hands, make eye contact, and introduce yourself.
- Remain confident and professional, but also personable.
- Mirror their speech and behavior.
- Begin with general questions and small talk.
- Show interest in them and their interests.
- Notice and comment on positives.
- Find some common ground on which to relate.

3. Discuss Needs + Wants

Once you have spent a few moments getting to know your prospect, start asking open-ended questions to discover some of their needs and wants. Ask what brought them to your agency. If you are meeting them to present a property or your service, ask why they are interested in, or what criteria they have in mind for that property.

- If you are making a sales presentation, ask for a few moments at the outset to outline the process of buying or seling, as well as how you have structured the presentation.
- Listen intently, and repeat back information you are not sure you understand.
- Ask open-ended questions to get them talking. The longer they talk, the more insight they are providing you into their needs and motivations.
- Ask clarifying questions about their responses.

4. Present the Solution

Once you have a solid understanding of what they are looking for, you can begin to present the solution: your service as a Realtor®.

- Explain how you can help them meet their objective.
- Illustrate your points with anecdotes about other happy clients, or awards the product or service has earned.
- Use hypothetical examples featuring your client. Encourage them to picture what it would be like to bring friends over to their new home.
- Begin by describing the benefits of your service as a Realtor®, then follow up with features and advantages.
- Watch your client's behavior as you speak, and ask further qualifying questions in response to body language and verbal comments.
- Give the client an opportunity to ask you questions or provide feedback about listing, buying or financing.
- Ask closed-ended questions to gain agreement.

5. Overcome Objections

As you present your service as a Realtor®, take note of potential objections by asking open-ended questions and monitoring body language. Expect that objections will arise and prepare for it. Consider brainstorming a list of all potential objections, and writing down your responses.

- Repeat the objection back to the client to ensure you understand them correctly.
- Empathize with what they have said, and then provide a response that overcomes the objection.
- Confirm that the answer you have provided has overcome their objection by repeating yourself.

Immediate Clients

The Eight Most Common Objections
Your service does not seem valuable to me. FSBO. There is no reason for me to act now. I will wait. It's safest not to make a decision right away. There is not enough money for the purchase. The competitor offers a better service or lower commission. There are internal issues between people or departments. The relationship with the decision maker is strained. There is an existing contract in place with another Realtor®.

6. Close

This is an important part of the sales process that should be handled delicately. Deciding when to close is a judgment call that must be made in the moment during the sale. Ideally, you have presented a solution to their needs, overcome objections, and have the client in a place where they are ready to engage you.

Here are some questions to ask before you close the sale:

- Does my prospect agree that there is value in my service?
- Does my prospect understand the features and benefits of using my service?
- Are there any remaining objections that must be handled?
- What other factors could influence my prospect's decision to buy?
- Have I minimized the risk involved in the contract, and provided some level of urgency?

Once you have determined it is time to make the sale, here are some sample statements you can use to get the process rolling:

- So, should we get started?
- Can I email you a draft contract tomorrow?

7. Service + Follow-up

Once you have made the closed on a property, your work is not over. You want to ensure that that client will become a loyal, repeat client, and that they will refer their friends to your business.

Ask them to be in your client database, and keep in touch with regular newsletters. Follow up with a phone call to ask how they are enjoying their new home, and if they have any further questions or needs you can assist them with.

This contact opportunity will also allow you ask for a referral. At the very least, it will ensure you are continuing to foster and build a relationship with the client.

Sales Team

Employing a team of strong salespeople

What Makes a Good Realtor®?

There are a lot of Realtors® out there – but what qualities and skills make a great salesperson? These are the attributes you will want to find or develop in your team:

- Willingness to continuously learn and improve sales skills
- Sincerity in relating to clients and providing solutions to their objectives
- An understanding of the company's big picture
- A communication style that is direct, polite, and professional
- Honesty and respect for other team members, clients, as well

as the competition.
- Ability to manage time
- Enthusiastic
- Inquisitive
- A great listener
- Ability to quickly interpret, analyze, and respond to information during the sales process
- Ability to connect and develop relationships of trust with potential clients
- Professional appearance

Team Building – Keeping Your Team Together

In many businesses, sales is a department or a whole team of people who work together to generate leads and convert clients. Effective management of your sales team is a skill every business owner should cultivate.

Teambuilding, recruitment, and training will be discussed in later sections, but take some time to consider the following aspects of managing a sales team:

Communication
- Are targets and results regularly reviewed?
- Are opportunities for input regularly provided?
- Do sales staff members have a clear understanding of what is expected?
- Do all staff members know, monthly and quarterly targets?

Performance Management

- Are sales staff members motivated to reach targets?
- Are sales staff recognized and rewarded once those targets are reached?
- Are there opportunities for skills training and development?
- Do staff members have broad and comprehensive industry knowledge?
- Is there opportunity for growth within the company?
- Is performance regularly reviewed?

Operations

- Do you have a solid understanding of your sales numbers (revenue, profit, margins)?
- Are your sales processes regularly reviewed?
- Do you have a variety of sales scripts prepared?
- Do you measure conversion rates?
- How are your leads generated?

Sales Tools

Every salesperson should have an arsenal of tools on hand to assist them in the sales process. These tools can act as aids while a sale is taking place, or help to foster continual learning and development of the salesperson's skills and approach.

The list below includes some popular sales tools. Add to this list with other resources that are specific to your business or industry.

Immediate Clients

Tool	Description + Benefit
Scripts	Used for incoming and outgoing telemarketing, getting listings, getting buyers, farming Create several different scripts throughout your business Maintains consistency in your sales approach Revise and renew your scripts regularly
Presentation Materials	High-quality information about the advantage of buying or selling with you Forms: PowerPoint presentation, brochure, property brochures, proposal Serves as an outline of your sales presentation, and keeps you on task
Colleagues	A source of help and advice, especially when you are on the same team or sell similar products Also a source of support
Client Databases	An accurate, up-to-date database of client contact information and contact history Used to stay in touch with clients Can also be used for direct mail and follow-up telemarketing
The Internet	A powerful resource for sales help and advice Information to help improve your sales process Online sales coaching Source for product knowledge
Ongoing Training	Constant improvement of your sales skills Constant increase in product knowledge Investment in yourself and your company

8 Tips for Better Sales

- **Dress for the sale.** Dress professionally, appear well put together and maintain good hygiene. Ensure you are not only dressed professionally, but *appropriately*. Would your client feel more comfortable if you wore a suit, or jeans and blazer?

- **Speak their language.** Show you understand their industry or culture, and use phrases your client understands. This may require researching industry jargon or common phrases. Remember to avoid using words and phrases that are used in the sales process: sold, contract, telemarketing, finance, interest, etc. Doing so will help break down the salesperson/client barrier.

- **Ooze positivity**. Show up or answer the phone with a smile, and leave your personal or business issues behind. Be enthusiastic about what you have to offer, and how that offering will benefit your client. Reflect this not only in your voice, but also in your body language.

- **Deliver a strong pitch or presentation**. Be confident and convincing. Leave self-doubt at the door, and walk in assuming the sale. Take time to explain complex concepts, and always connect what you're saying to your audience in a specific way.

- **Be a poster-child for good manners**. Accept any amenity you're offered, listen intently, don't interrupt, don't show up late, have a strong handshake, and give everyone you are speaking to equal attention.

Immediate Clients

- **Avoid sensitive subjects**. Politics, religion, swearing, sexual innuendos and racial comments are absolutely off-limits. So are negative comments about other clients or the competition.
- **Create a real relationship.** Icebreakers and small talk are not just to pass the time before your presentation. They are how relationships get established. Show genuine interest in everything your client has to say. Ask questions about topics you know they are passionate. Speak person to person, not salesperson to client. Remember everything.
- **Know more than you need to.** Impress clients with comprehensive knowledge – not only of you're the properties in your market – but also of real estate trends and financing. Be seen as an expert in order to build trust and respect.

4

Double Your Referrals

What if I told you that you could put an inexpensive system in place that would effectively allow your business to growth itself?

For most business owners, a large part of their client base is comprised of referral clients. These people found out about the company's services from the recommendation of a friend or colleague who had a positive experience purchasing from that company. This can be especially profitable for a real estate ageny.

If your business benefits from referral clients, you will find that these clients arrive ready to do business with you. They also tend to be highly loyal to your company.

Seem like great clients to have, don't they?

Referral clients cost less to acquire. Compared to the leads you generate from advertising, direct mail campaigns, and other marketing initiatives, referral clients come to you already qualified and already trusting in the quality of your offering and the respectability of your staff.

With a little effort, and the creation of a formalized system – or strategy – you can not only continue to enjoy referral business, but easily double the number of referral clients that walk through your door. All of this is possible for a minimal investment of time and resources.

Is Your Business a Referral Business?

Referral based businesses benefit from a stream of qualified clients who arrive at their doorstep ready to list or buy. These businesses put less focus on advertising to generate new leads, and more focus on serving and communicating with their existing clients.

Generally speaking, a referral program can generate outstanding results for nearly any business. Since most referrals do not require any effort, the addition of a strategy and a program will often double or triple the number of qualified referrals that come through a business door.

A referral program can:

- **Save you time**. Referral strategies – once established – don't require much management or time investment.
- **Deliver more qualified clients**. Your client arrives with an assumption of trust, and willing to purchase.
- **Improve your reputation.** Your client's networks likely overlap, and create potential for a single client to be referred by two people. This encourages the perception that your business is "the place to go."
- **Speed the sales process.** You will have existing common ground and a reputation with the referred client.

- **Increase your profit.** You will spend less time and money generating leads, and more time serving clients who have their wallets open.

The Cost of Your Clients

As we discussed in the "Repeat Business" section, you don't "get" clients, you *buy* them. The money you spend on advertising, direct mail, and other promotions ideally results in potential clients walking through your doors.

For example, if you placed an ad for $200, and 4 people list or buy their properties with you, to that ad, you would have paid $50 for each client.

Referral clients cost you next to nothing. Your existing client does the work of selling your business to their friend or associate, and you benefit from the sale. Aside from the cost of any referral incentives or coupon production, there is no cost involved at all.

Referral clients cost less and require less time investment than any other client. That means you can spend that time making them a loyal client, or a devoted fan.

Groom Your Clients

Referral strategies can allow you to groom your client base. As we have previously discussed, 80% of your revenue comes from 20% of your clients – these are your ideal clients.

These are also the people you have established as your target market, and are the people you cater your marketing and advertising efforts toward.

You also have a group of clients who make up 80% of your

headaches. These are the people who complain the most and profit you the least.

Use your referral strategy to get more of your *ideal* clients. Spend more time servicing your ideal clients – do everything you can to make them happy – and less time on your headache clients. You can even ask your headache clients to go elsewhere.

Then, focus your referral efforts on your ideal clients. Ask them to refer business to you, and reward them for doing so. Try to avoid referrals from your headache clients – chances are you'll just get another headache.

Referral Sources

Take some time to brainstorm all the people who could potentially refer business to you. Think beyond your business, to your extracurricular activities and personal life. There are endless sources of people who are ready and willing to send potential clients your way.

Here are some ideas to get you started:

Past Relationships

No, not romantic relationships. I'm talking about anyone you have previously had a relationship with, but for one reason or another have fallen out of touch. This includes former colleagues, associates, clients and friends.

Including them in your referral strategy can be as simple as reaching out through the phone or email, and updating them on your latest business initiative or career move. Gently ask at the end of the correspondence to refer anyone who may need your product or service. They will appreciate that you have attempted to re-establish the relationship.

Suppliers and Vendors

Your suppliers and vendors can be a great source for referrals, because they presumably deal daily with businesses that are complementary to your own. The opportunities to connect two of their clients in a mutually beneficial relationship are endless. These businesses should be happy to help out - especially if you have been a regular and loyal client.

Clients

Clients are an obvious source of referrals because they are the people who are dealing with you directly on a regular basis. Often, all you have to do is ask and they will happily provide you with contact information of other interested buyers, or contact those buyers themselves.

Your clients also have a high level of product knowledge when it comes to your business, and are in a great position to really sell the strength of your company. Remember from the Testimonials section, the words of your clients are at least 10 times more powerful than any clever headline or marketing piece you could create.

Employees and Associates

Give your employees and associates a reason to have their friends and families do business with you with a simple incentive program. These people have the most industry knowledge, and are in the best position to sell you to a potential client.

This is also a way to tap into an endless network of people.

Who do your employees and associates know? Who do their friends and friends of friends know? A referral chain that connects to your employees can be a highly powerful one.

Competitors

This doesn't seem so obvious, but it can work. Your direct competitors are clearly not the ideal source for referrals. However, indirect competitors can refer their clients or potential clients to you if they cannot meet those clients' needs themselves.

For example, if you sell out-of-State investment properties and your competitor down the street doesn't, you can offer a finder's fee or commission split to establish this arrangement.

Your Network

Don't be shy about asking your friends and family members for referrals. Too many people do not provide enough information to their inner circle about what they do or what their business does. This doesn't make sense, since these are the people who should be the most interested!

Take time to explain clearly what your business is all about, and what your point of difference is. Then just ask them if they know anyone who may benefit from what you are offering. You could even provide your friends and family with an incentive – a gift, a meal, or a finder's fee, if that is allowed in your State..

Associations + Special Interest Groups

This is another place you likely have a network of people who have limited knowledge about what you do or what your business does. The advantage here is that you have a group of people with similar belief s and values in the same room. Use it!

The Media

Unless a member of the media is a regular client of yours, or you are in business to serve the media, this may not seem like an obvious choice either.

The opportunity here is to establish a relationship with an editor or journalist, and position yourself as an expert in your field or industry. Then, next time they are writing a related story, they can ask to quote you and your opinion. When their audience reads the story, they will perceive your business as the industry leader.

Referral Strategies

A referral strategy is any system you can put in place to generate new leads through existing clients. The ideal way to do this is to create a system that runs itself! Here are some ideas for simple strategies you can begin to implement into your business immediately.

Just Ask

This may seem simple and obvious, but it's true. Be open with your clients and associates, and simply ask them if they can refer any of their friends or associates to you. Make it part of doing business with you, and your clients will grow to expect the question. Or, let them know in advance that you'll be asking at a later date.

Remember that this can include potential clients – even if they don't buy from you. The reason they chose not to purchase may have nothing to do with your business; any person who has begun to or actually done business with you can refer to you another person.

Offer Incentives

When you speak to your clients, when you ask them for something, you typically try to answer the question "what's in it for me?" before they ask it.

The same is true when you ask your clients for a referral. Incentive-based referral strategies work wonders, and can easily be implemented as part of a client loyalty program, or as part of your existing client relations systems.

Consider offering clients who successfully refer clients to you incentives, such as gifts. Offer incentives relative to the number of referrals, or the success rate of each referral.

This can have a spin off effect, as your referral clients may become motivated to continue the referral chain. They too will be interested in the incentives you have provided, and tell their friends about your business.

Be Proactive

The only way your referral program will work is if you put some effort into it, and maintain some level of ongoing effort.

Here are some ideas:

- Put a referral card or coupon in every mailing and advertising piece.
- Offer free information seminars to existing clients, and ask them to bring a friend

Provide Great Client Service

An easy way to encourage referral business is to treat every potential client with exemplary client service. Since the art of client service is lost is many communities, people are often impressed by simple added touches and conveniences. That alone will encourage them to refer your business to their network.

Stay in Touch

Make sure you are staying in touch with all of your potential and converted clients. Through newsletters, direct mail, promotional products or the Internet, keep your business name at the top of the minds, ahead of the competition.

Even if they have already purchased from you, and may not need to purchase for some time, a newsletter or email can be a simple reminder that your business is out there. If someone in their network is looking for the product or service, it will be more likely that your client will refer your business over the competition.

5

Profit Over the Phone

For some, the word 'telemarketing' brings up images of rows of people with headsets, all working from a head office in a country far, far away.

Others think of the people who always seem to call the minute they take their first bite of dinner. Some just think it's an old fashioned marketing strategy. While in some cases this may be true, telemarketing is still an important tool for every business – of every size.

What if I were to tell you that you were *already* using telemarketing as a regular part of your business? In fact, telemarketing is re-emerging as a powerful way to generate leads and close sales. Done well, it's also efficient and cost-effective.

Every time the people who work your front end pick up the phone, they're engaging in a telemarketing process. Every time one of your salespeople picks up the phone, they too are engaging in a telemarketing process.

Telemarketing is not just a system for cold calls. It's any type of formal communication between you or your company and its clients over the phone.

So, now you know that you're already doing it, let's talk

about how to turn telemarketing into a profitable marketing strategy for your business.

Telemarketing for Your Real Estate Business

A common misconception is that telemarketing needs to happen on a broad scale in order to be effective. Pages and pages of potential clients must be cold called on a daily basis. Businesses must hire dozens of staff members to conduct and manage the efforts.

As I mentioned above, telemarketing is any kind of formal communication that happens between a company and a potential or existing client over the phone. Regardless of the size of your business, you can train you existing staff members to effectively use the telephone to generate more leads and convert more sales.

The benefits of establishing an organized telemarketing system are:

- Instant access. Reach key prospects immediately.
- One-on-one interaction. Develop real relationships with empathy and trust.
- Minimal cost. Spend less on sales outreach and research.

Who are the Best Telemarketers?

Success in telemarketing has a lot to do with the personality of your company's representative. Generally, good telemarketers have the following qualities and abilities:

- Energy and enthusiasm
- Positive attitude
- Good phone manner
- Empathy

- Belief in your company and its products
- Strong listening skills
- Ability to think on-the-spot
- Ability to handle objection and rejection
- Good organizational skills

The Telemarketing Process

There are two types of telemarketing: outgoing and incoming. You should have a proactive strategy in place to handle both types.

Remember that your approach to telemarketing must have a clear objective; a clear purpose. What is the purpose of the call (outgoing and incoming)? Is it to inform? Set up an appointment? Establish a need or desire? This will help guide how you handle each type.

Incoming Calls

When a client calls your business for the first time, you should have a system in place to make a great, client service-oriented impression. Many of these clients will have seen one of your advertisements, received a direct mail piece, or be responding to any other element of your marketing campaign.

Your telemarketing strategy for incoming phone calls can take the form of:

- An answering service
- Voice mail
- A messaging service
- An order taking system

- An information provision system

The person – or people – who answer incoming calls should be well trained for the role and clearly understand the expectations for handling them. Your receptionist should be trained thoroughly in your market so he can answer basic client questions intelligently. Your team should know how to answer the phone according to your company policy, and have excellent phone manners.

Consider including the following instructions into your incoming telemarketing system or process:

- Answer the phone after two and before four rings
- Have a standard company greeting. Include your company name, as well as the name of the person answering the phone.
- Ensure sufficient client information is recorded. Determine what information is important to gain from each caller – name, phone number, reason for call, action required, who is responsible for following up
- Do not place anyone on hold for longer than 20 seconds. Instead, take their name and number and have their call returned promptly.
- Establish a short description of your company's process or point of difference at some point during the phone call.
- Always repeat back any information or agreement exchanged.
- Be the last one to hang up.

Outgoing Calls

Outgoing calls are the more challenging aspect of your telemarketing strategy. In this case you are proactively asking your client for something, as opposed to responding once they've already been convinced to act.

You can use an outgoing telemarketing strategy to:

- Set appointments
- Generate leads
- Make cold calls
- Update databases
- Follow up on direct mail and other campaigns
- Convert leads to sales
- Conduct surveys

Your outgoing phone call needs to engage the person on the other end, and begin to build a relationship based solely on verbal communication (i.e., without the assistance of non-verbal cues and behaviors). Depending on the type of call, you will be seeking to:

- Attract their attention
- Spark their interest, needs, or desires
- Motivate them to act
- Seek agreement

It is essential to the success of your outgoing telemarketing efforts that you create a script for each type of outgoing call your company makes. This will keep you – and your staff – focused on the purpose of the call and give you tools and prompts to keep you on track. We will review scripts for telemarketing later in this chapter.

Here are some simple steps for making your outgoing telemarketing efforts a success:

Know who you are calling

Do your research. If you are calling a business, know exactly who it is you need to contact. Is it the manager or vice-president? Owner or CEO? Once you know who you are targeting, you can do some research prior to your phone call, and ensure you call at a time that is convenient. You will want to know a bit about their industry and the type of properties suitable for them as well as the company and their role within it. If you have served another client in the same industry, let them know.

When you have them on the phone, confirm that the basic information you have is correct (name, title, etc.). If you do not know who the best person to speak to is, ask the receptionist for the name of the person who makes real estate decisions.

Be prepared; stay organized

Have all the materials you may need in front of you, and clear your desk of any distractions. Have a notepad handy, and record key elements of the conversation for action or later discussion. Also, keep a record of all the calls you make, and the results of each call. This will prevent you from making duplicate calls, which do not reflect well on you or your organization, as well as track left messages and the most productive times of the day for outgoing phone calls.

Know why you are calling

As I mentioned above, your phone calls should be purpose-focused. Are you calling to set up a meeting? Introduce yourself and your products? Get them to try what you have to offer? Keep this clear in your mind and stick to it.

Get past the gatekeeper

To reach busy decision makers, you will have to get past the person who screens unsolicited phone calls when you are calling a business: The gatekeeper is usually an assistant, or secretary. Do not assume you will be able to speak to your prospect with the first phone call – it may take two, three, or even seven tries until you are successful. Here are some guidelines for developing a relationship with the gatekeeper:

- Ask for their name and write it down
- Do not underestimate the power of developing a relationship with them
- Get an understanding of their position and responsibilities
- Stay positive and confident
- Never pitch the receptionist
- Once you have developed a relationship, ask them to help you pin the decision-maker down

Be persistent

Persistence pays off – especially when it comes to large potential accounts. You may have to call many times before you can work your way through the gatekeeper, to the person you wish to speak to. Expect this, stay positive, and your persistence will pay off.

Use strong phone skills

You can create a great first impression on the phone when

you cultivate great phone communication skills. Pay attention to the tone of your voice, whether or not you are smiling, the pacing of your sentences (slower is better), and general phone manners. Ensure you clearly identify who you are and what company you work for every time you speak to someone new.

Telemarketing Scripts

Scripts are essential to successful telemarketing. You and your employees will benefit having a "plan of action" for every type of phone call that your company makes. This will also ensure that each staff member has a consistent approach, which is part of your branding.

We discussed the importance of scripts and writing scripts earlier in the program, but I encourage you to review the section before you craft your telemarketing scripts.

Here is a list of components you will need to include in your scripts:

Greeting: Opening the Conversation

Your incoming calls should be handled with a consistent, friendly greeting that informs the client of what company (or department) they've reached and who they're talking to.

Outgoing calls need to engage the client within the first few moments, just as a headline needs to catch the reader's instant attention. Say just enough to pique their interest and keep them listening, then begin to explain why you are calling.

The opening conversation should be simple and focused on developing a relationship. Ask casual questions and use small talk to put the caller at ease, but don't go on too long. You don't want to appear to be wasting their time.

Reason for your Call

If someone asks why you are calling, tell them. Be up front about why you are calling; clearly state your objectives, then back them up with an explanation that includes benefits to the client.

You may wish to ask permission before you get into an explanation. Asking, "do you mind if I tell you exactly why I called today?" shows respect for the client's time, and gives them an opportunity to agree to listen.

You may also wish to outline exactly what you're going to cover during the call. Again, ask them if you can go over this information with them. This will show that you have given the phone call substantial thought, organized your information, and respect their time.

Asking Questions

Information gathering is an essential component of both incoming and outgoing telemarketing. Ask as many questions as possible, and encourage your client to start talking. This will keep you in control of the conversation. Even if these questions don't relate specifically to the product, your client will provide firsthand information that you can add to your market research.

For incoming calls, listen to the client's question, then ask if you can take a moment to ask them some questions before you answer theirs. This will allow you to explain your company's process, ask the client some qualifying questions, and gain control of the conversation.

You will want to also consider asking questions related to the following topics:

- **Responsibility** – Who is in charge of making the decision? Is it the same person who will be finalizing the deal?
- **Budget** – How much financial resources are available for your proposal? What is the budget? What influences this number? Will they need financing?
- **Timeframe** – When does the client need the to make a move? What is the reason for these deadlines?
- **Competition** – Who else is the client talking to? What will impact their decision? What aspects are they comparing?

Closed-ended questions

Closed-ended questions are not the best way to get your client talking, but they do provide information quickly and succinctly. Closed-ended questions are questions that can be answered with one word – usually yes or no.

Open-ended questions

Open-ended questions are just that: they cannot be answered in one word. These are great questions to use for the majority of your telemarketing because they encourage the client to provide explanations, giving you insight into their needs and opinions.

Obtaining Agreement

At key points throughout the conversation, you will need to ensure you are on the same page as your client. You will need to find a way to get some feedback from your caller on what you have been saying.

An easy way to do this is to ask them a question you are sure they'll say yes to. Something like, "so as you can see, it's a pretty irresistible offer."

Encouraging them to agree with you strengthens your argument, and leads directly to the sale. It's a powerful method of persuasion.

Overcoming Objections

This will be the most challenging component of your script – largely because you do not know for sure what your client's objections are going to be. You will have to think in the moment, and attempt to overcome each objection in a calm, professional way.

Before you pick up the phone, you may wish to brainstorm all potential objections, and think of your ideal response. A simple chart that looks like this will be a helpful tool to refer to during your call:

Potential Objection	**Response**

Remember to respect the objections as they are raised, and treat each point your client makes as a legitimate one. Show empathy and relate to what they have to say. Phrases like "I can see how that would be a concern for you…" "I used to think the same thing…" and "Sure, that's completely understandable…" allow you to relate to them, establish common ground, and then share how you overcame your own objections.

Closing with Commitment

Once you have opened the conversation, developed a relationship, asked questions, secured agreement, and overcome objections, all you have to do is close the conversation with a commitment.

The commitment should be your objective for calling, or a step toward that objective. For example, if the purpose of your call was to set up a meeting, ensure that you commit to a time and place before you end the conversation. Since choosing a Realtor® to use in buying or selling real estate is a major decision, you may have to make a few phone calls or hold a few appointments to achieve that.

Assume that if you have got this far, you have the sale. Be confident, and use phrases like, "How about we meet on this day at this time…" and "Where can I send the information?"

You will want to confirm whatever you have committed to in writing with your client. If you have set an appointment, send them a quick note to thank them for the phone call, and put the meeting in writing. Remember to be as polite and succinct as possible. Avoid lengthy emails and letters.

Tips for Effective Telemarketing

Communicating with your existing and potential clients over the phone requires a different set of skills than in-person communication. If you do not make the calls yourself, make sure you choose the best people for this job – when you only have your voice to communicate, you must be extra aware of the impression you give the person on the other line.

Smile

This may seem like a silly point to put at the top of this list, but it is important. Your caller will be able to hear if you are smiling, and interpret your smile as enthusiasm. You will sound more positive, friendly, and open to dialogue. Remember, the person on the other line can hear *everything*, so avoid multi-tasking (drinking, eating, unnecessary typing) when you're on the phone.

Be a good listener

Once you get your client talking – listen. They will be giving you important insight into their purchase motivations, and their potential objections. Take notes as you listen, and never assume you know what they are going to say. After long periods of speech, check in and repeat back what you have heard to confirm you have heard it properly. Make sure to leave a pause between what they have just said, and what you are about to say. This shows that you have been listening and are not jumping in at your first opportunity.

Call at an optimal time

Knowing who you are calling will ensure that you contact them at the most appropriate time – the time they are most likely to answer you phone call. For example, business owners will need to be reached during business hours. Try to reach them during quiet times – usually first thing in the morning, or right before close. If you are calling individuals about residential properties, then make your calls in the evening when they are most likely to be home.

Use a familiar tone

You only have your voice to establish a new relationship with a potential client. The tone you choose is just as important – and has just as much impact – as the words you choose. Use a tone that is friendly and confident, and resembles the way you would speak to your friends.

Be prepared to handle rejection

No matter how targeted your contact list, how amazing your script, how great your approach, rejection is an inevitable part of outgoing telemarketing. Your telemarketers are going to have to become very skilled at handling rejection. In fact, some people will not only reject what you have to say, they'll be rude in doing so. Remember not to take this personally – they could be having a bad day, or just not have enough time to listen to what you have to say. Consider asking to call back at a better time – or just shrug it off.

Be prepared to handle difficult clients

Difficult clients will appear on the other end of the phone line – for both incoming and outgoing calls. This is another inevitability of telemarketing, and business in general. Again, remember not to take what they have to say personally – they just want to air their frustrations and be heard. Listen intently, stay calm, and try to empathize with what they have to say. Never interrupt, use calming language, and record as much as possible about what they are saying. Then, either promise to follow up – allowing yourself to take time to consider how you would like to handle the problem – to try to resolve their issue immediately.

Make the call standing up

When you are standing, you will sound more confident, authoritative, and decisive. Your diaphragm is expanded when you are standing, which will increase the confidence in your voice. Do this for the important phone calls – the big accounts.

Have strong phone manners

Here are some tips for ensuring you have a strong, professional phone presence:

- Ask for the contact by name, not role title
- Use your full name when asked who is calling
- Clearly state your company name
- Tell them why you are calling
- If you do not reach your client, ask for a more convenient time

Do not hold, call back instead (your time is valuable, too!)

6

Generate Unlimited Leads

Where do your clients come from?

Most people would probably choose advertising as an answer. Or referrals. Or direct mail campaigns. This may seem true, but it's not really accurate.

Your clients come from leads that have been turned into sales. Each client goes through a two-step process before they arrive ready to do business with you. They have been converted from a member of a target market, to a lead, then to a client.

So, would it not stand to reason then, that when you advertise or send any marketing material out to your target market, that you're not really trying to generate clients? That instead, you're trying to generate leads.

When you look at your marketing campaign from this perspective, the idea of generating leads as compared to clients seems a lot less daunting. The pressure of closing sales is no longer placed on advertisements or brochures.

From this perspective, the **general purpose of your advertising and marketing efforts is then to generate leads from qualified clients.** Seems easy enough, doesn't it?

Where Are Your Leads Coming From?

If I asked you to tell me the top three ways you generate new sales leads, what would you say?

- Advertising?
- Word of mouth?
- Networking?
- don't know?

The first step toward increasing your leads is in understanding how many leads you currently get on a regular basis, as well as where they come from. Otherwise, how will you know when you're getting more phone calls or walk-in clients?

If you don't know where your leads come from, start *today*. Start asking every client that comes to you, "how did you hear about us?" or "what brought you in today?" Ask every client that calls where they found your telephone number, or email address. Then, *record the information for at least an entire week.*

When you're finished, take a look at your spreadsheet and write your top three lead generators here:

1. _____

2. _____

3. _____

From Lead to Client: Conversion Rates

Leads mean nothing to your business unless you convert them into clients. You could get hundreds of leads from a single advertisement, but unless those leads result in clients, it's been a largely unsuccessful (and costly) campaign.

The ratio of leads (potential clients) to transactions (actual clients) is called your conversion rate. Simply divide the number of clients who actually became clients by the number of prospects who inquired about your product or service, and multiply by 100.

 # transactions / # leads x 100 = % conversion rate

If, in a given week, I have 88 clients contact my real estate office, and 14 of them contract to list or purchase a property, the formula would look like this:

[14 (clients) / 88 (leads)] x 100 = 16.25% conversion rate

What's Your Conversion Rate?

Based on the formula above, you can see that the higher your conversion rate, the more profitable the business.

Your next step is to determine you own current conversion rate. Add up the number of leads you sourced in the last section, and divide that number into the total transactions that took place in the same week.

Write your conversion rate here:

_____.

Quality (or Qualified) Leads

Based on our review of conversion rates, we can see that the number of leads you generate means nothing unless those leads are being converted into clients.

So what affects your ability (and the ability of your team) to turn leads into clients? Do you need to improve your scripts? Your service? Find a more competitive edge in the marketplace?

Maybe. But the first step toward increasing conversion rates is to evaluate the leads you are currently generating, and make sure those leads are the right ones.

What are Quality Leads?

Potential clients are potential clients, right? Anyone who walks into your office or picks up the phone to call your business could be convinced to purchase from you, right? Not necessarily, but this is a common assumption most business owners make.

Quality leads are the people who are the most likely to buy your product or service. They are the qualified buyers who comprise your target market. Anyone might walk in off the street to ask about properties– regardless of whether or not they are in the market to buy or sell their home or other property. This lead is solely interested in browsing, and is not likely to be converted to a client.

A quality lead would be someone looking for a new home, and who specifically comes to you because a friend had raved about the service they received from you. **These are the kinds of leads you need to focus on generating.**

How Do You Get Quality Leads?

- **Know your target market**. Get a handle on who your clients are – the people who are most likely to buy or list a property. Know their age, sex, income, and purchase motivations. From that information you can determine how best to reach your specific audience.
- **Focus on the 80/20 rule.** A common statistic in business is that 80% of your revenue comes from 20% of your clients. These are your star clients, or your ideal clients. These are the clients you should focus your efforts on recruiting. This is the easiest way to grow your business and your income.
- **Get specific.** Focus not only on who you want to attract, but how you're going to attract them. If you're trying to generate leads from a specific market segment, craft a unique offer to get their attention.
- **Be proactive**. Once you've generated a slew of leads, make sure you have the resources to follow up on them. Be diligent and aggressive, and follow up in a timely manner. You've done to work to get them, now reel them in.

Get More Leads from Your Existing Strategies

Increasing your lead generation doesn't necessarily mean diving in and implementing an expensive array of new marketing strategies. Marketing and client outreach for the purpose of lead generation can be inexpensive, and bring a high return on investment.

You are likely already implementing many of these strategies. With a little tweaking or refinement, you can easily double your leads, and ensure they are more qualified.

Here are some popular ways to generate quality leads:

Direct Mail to Your Ideal Clients

Direct mail is one of the fastest and most effective ways to generate leads that will build your business. It's a simple strategy.

The secret to doubling your results is to craft your direct mail campaigns specifically for a highly targeted audience of your *ideal* clients.

Your ideal clients are the people who will are likely in the market to buy or sell their home or commercial property. They are the clients who could possibly buy or list with you over and over again, and refer your business to their friends. They are the group of 20% of your clients who make up 80% of your revenue.

Identify your ideal clients

Who are your ideal clients? What is their age, sex, income, location and purchase motivation? Where do they live? How do they spend their money? Be as specific as possible.

Once you have identified who your ideal clients are, you can begin to determine how you can go about reaching them. Will you mail to households or businesses? Families or retirees? Direct mail lists are available for purchase from a wide range of companies, and can be segregated into a variety of demographic and sociographic categories.

Generate Unlimited Leads

Craft a special offer

Create an offer that's too good to refuse – not for your entire target market, but for your ideal client. How can you cater to their unique needs and wants? What will be irresistible for them?

For example, if you specialize in mid-range residential properites or starter homes, your target market is a broad range of people. However, if you are targeting vacation properties to uppp-income people, your target audience and your offer will be much different.

Court them for their business

Don't stop at a single mail-out. Sometimes people will throw your letter away two or three times before they are motivated to act. Treat your direct mail campaign like a courtship, and understand that it will happen over time.

First send a letter introducing yourself, and your irresistible offer. Then follow up on a monthly basis with additional letters, newsletters, offers, or flyers. Repetition and reinforcement of your presence is how your client will go from saying, "who is this Realtor® or company" to "I buy from this Realtor® or company."

Advertise for lead generation

Statistics show that nearly 50% of all purchase decisions are motivated by advertising. It can also be a relatively cost effective way of generating leads.

We've already discussed the importance of ensuring your advertisements are purpose-focused. The general purpose of most advertisements is to increase sales – which starts with leads. However ads that are created solely for lead generation – that is, to get the clients to pick up the phone or walk into the office – are a category of their own.

Lead generation ads are simply designed and create a sense of curiosity or mystery. Often, they feature an almost unbelievable offer. Their purpose is not to convince the client to buy, but to contact the Realtor® or office for more information.

As always, when you are targeting your ideal audience, you'll need to ensure that your ads are placed prominently in publications that audience reads. This doesn't mean you have to fork over the cash for expensive display ads. Inexpensive advertising in e-mail newsletters, classifieds, and the Internet are very effective for lead generation.

Here are some tips for lead generation advertising:

Leverage low-cost advertising

Place ads in, classifieds section, e-mail newsletters, and online. If your target audience is technology savvy, consider new forms of advertising like Facebook and Google Adwords.

Spark curiosity

Don't give them all the information they need to make a decision. Ask them to contact you for the full story, or the complete details of the seemingly outrageous offer.

Grab them with a killer headline

Like all advertising, a compelling headline is essential. Focus on the greatest benefits to the client, or feature an unbelievable offer.

Referrals and host beneficiary relationships

A referral system is one of the most profitable systems you can create in your business. The beauty is once it's set up, it often runs itself.

Clients that come to you through referrals are often your "ideal clients." They are already trusting and willing to buy. This is one of the most cost-effective methods of generating new business, and is often the most profitable. These referral clients will buy more, faster, and refer further business to your company.

Referrals naturally happen without much effort for reputable businesses, but with a proactive referral strategy you'll certainly double or triple your referrals. Sometimes, you just need to ask!

Here are some easy strategies you can begin to implement today:

Referral incentives

Give your clients a reason to refer business to you. Reward them with a restaurant gift card or other gift in exchange for a successful referral.

Referral program

Offer new clients a free product or service to get them in the door. Then, at the end of the transaction, give them three more 'coupons' for the same free product or service that they can give to their friends. Do the same with their friends. This ongoing program will bring you more business than you can imagine.

Host-beneficiary relationships

Forge alliances with non-competitive companies who target your ideal clients. Create cross-promotion and cross-referral direct mail campaigns that benefit both businesses.

Lead Management Systems

Once your lead generation strategies are in place, you'll also need a system to manage incoming inquiries. You'll need to ensure you receive enough information from each lead to follow up on at a later date. You'll also need to create a system to organize that information, and track the lead as it is converted into a sale.

Gathering Information from Your Leads

Here is a list of information you should gather from your leads. This list can be customized to the needs of your business, and the type of information you can realistically ask for from your potential clients.

• Company Name	• Cell Phone
• Name of Contact	• Email Address
• Alternate Contact Person	• Website Address
• Mailing Address	• Product of Interest
• Phone Number	• Other Competitors Engage
• Fax Number	

Lead List Management Methods:

Once you have gathered information from your lead, you'll need a system to organize their information and keep a detailed contact history.

The simplest way to do this is with a database program, but you can also use a variety of hard copy methods.

Electronic Database Programs

- High level of organization available
- Unlimited space for notes and record-keeping

Generate Unlimited Leads

- Data-entry required
- Examples include: MS Outlook, MS Excel, Maximizer
- Client Relationship Management Software

Index Cards

- Variety of sizes: 3x5, 4X6 or 5X8
- Basic contact information on one side
- Notes on the other side
- Easy to organize and sort

Rolodex System

- Maintain more contacts than index card system
- Easily organized and compact
- Basic contact information on one side
- Notes on the other side
- Can keep phone conversation and property details

Notebook

- Best if leads are managed by a single person
- Lots of room for notes
- Inexpensive
- Difficult to re-organize
- Best for smaller lists

Business Card Organizer

- Best for small lists – under 100
- Limited space for notes
- No data entry required
- Rolodex-style, or clear binder pages

7

Profits and Leads through Host-Beneficiary Relationships

Did you know that a business just down the street from yours may be able to help double your profits this year? Or does this sound a little too far-fetched?

Maybe. If you operate a retail store that sells tires, and the business down the road is a hair salon, you may have a hard time making this happen. However, loose partnerships between complementary, non-competing businesses can be a financial goldmine when implemented strategically. And your partner may be just steps away!

Formally called Host Beneficiary Relationships, these partnerships help small and medium-sized businesses tap into very specific target markets and close sales under existing relationships of trust.

HB Relationships allow one business (the 'host') to add value to their product or service, and the other (the 'beneficiary') to benefit from the impact of a referral. The beauty of this arrangement is that the roles can then be swapped; the 'host' becomes the 'beneficiary' and vice versa.

Like any marketing strategy, HB Relationships don't work for every business all the time. However, they are a great tool to keep in your marketing arsenal when starting a business, entering new markets, boosting product sales, or any other opportunity that requires a specific and personal approach.

How Can a HB Relationship Help Your Business?

Establishing, planning, and implementing a successful HB Relationship campaign is more complex than asking your neighbor to send a letter to his client base with an offer from your company.

As with every other component of your marketing strategy and materials, an HB Relationship campaign must be purpose-driven and evaluated to be the best approach to secure your desired results.

Depending on the regulations in your State, you could possibly seek an HB relationship with mortgage brokers, escrow companies, property insurance agents and other professionals who serve homeowners and business property owners.

So in what cases will a Host Beneficiary Relationship benefit your business?

1. A Start-up Company

A company that is just starting out has the most to gain from a HB Relationship. Faced with the standard challenges of establishing a new operation – credibility, product positioning, target

Profits and Leads through Host-Beneficiary Relationships

market establishment, marketing strategy, etc. – a HB Relationship is an ideal way to get the business off the ground.

Gaining access to a time-crafted list of potential clients in your target market is an impressive benefit. Getting an established business to communicate your offer on your behalf is an almost guaranteed way to establish your own credibility.

However, start-ups often have the least to offer a 'host' company in exchange for being the 'beneficiary'. Trading client lists is not an option in this case. So what's in it for the 'host'?

The host is seen in the eyes of his clients as providing a reward or an exclusive offer for their continued support and loyalty. The host business earns goodwill and has an excuse to contact his database for the cost of a simple mailing.

2. Entering a New Market

An established business venturing into new territory is in a prime position to benefit from a HB Relationship. Whether the business is known or unknown in the community, tapping into a refined target list will ensure that the right people are communicated the benefits of the new business' offering.

In exchange, the host business may benefit from either the beneficiary's client lists in other marketplaces, or the prestige of offering clients an exclusive offer for a new business in town.

Again, this works best when the target market is highly segmented; otherwise, an advertisement would be a faster and more cost effective strategy.

3. A New Product / Service

As with new marketplaces, launching a new product or service may require tapping into a new or more segmented audience to deliver your message. A HB Relationship with the right partner will help to correctly position your offering, and deliver it to an exact audience.

The host business benefits by offering loyal clients the first opportunity to purchase or use the beneficiary business' product or service.

Defining Your Target Market

This is crucial in establishing a HB Relationship – just like it is crucial in every other aspect of your marketing plan. Not knowing and understanding your target market will put you on the fast track to business hardship, and waste time and money in the process.

You can determine your target market – or target market segment – based on the purpose or intention for seeking a HB Relationship. Are you reaching out to a new segment of your market? Are you expanding into a new market area and looking to establish yourself amongst your broader target?

Determine your audience and write your target market here:

_____

_____

_____

Selecting a Host Business

Once you have an idea of who your target market is, you can begin to create a list of target host businesses to approach.

Not every business is going to be interested or willing to engage in this marketing strategy – so doing a little bit of research and positioning your offer is well worth your while. To begin, you will want to draft a long list of all potential host businesses.

Do this by considering all business types that would be complementary to – but not competing with – your business.

Those businesses that offer a service or product that is connected in some way to your own. For example, potential HB partners could be any type of business that deals with property owners – especially during the times they are considering buying, selling or leasing property..

Pick up the yellow pages (if you still have one), or conduct a Google search for all businesses in your market area that fall under the categories you identified. You may also consider asking your colleagues and associates for ideas and recommendations.

When creating this list, make sure each business falls under these criteria:

Non-competitive. Their offer should be complementary to, but not compete with, your product or service. Make sure you consider this carefully – seemingly non-competitive offers may actually cannibalize your business.

Same target market. If you and your host business are not talking to the same client base, then you're wasting your words on clients who are not likely to buy your service or product. If your host business has no idea who their target market is, you may also want to consider looking at other host options.

Start with your clients – your target market or segment of. What services do they use? What products are they interested in? Thinking about their needs will help lead you to the most effective host business.

A killer client contact list. Without this, they aren't worth approaching – but how do you know they have or maintain a client database? There are a couple of ways. Pay attention to the type of marketing your potential host conducts. Do they often send letters to their target market? Direct-mail flyers and other promotional materials? Or do they rely on advertising? Do they send a regular newsletter? They also may hold their client contact information in their point of sale system – if it is technologically advanced enough to do so.

Positive reputation. As the beneficiary, you need to ensure that the host who is referring your business to their clients enjoys a good reputation in the community and with its clientele. Otherwise, you are being endorsed by a business that no one respects, which can be damaging for your reputation.

Profits and Leads through Host-Beneficiary Relationships

Host Business Ideas List

Keep track of all potential host businesses using this chart.

Business Name	Contact	Business Type
	Name: Phone:	
	Name: Phone:	
	Name: Phone:	
	Name: Phone:	
	Name: Phone:	
	Name: Phone:	
	Name: Phone:	
	Name: Phone:	

Approaching the Host Business

Once you have created a list of target businesses, it is time to plan your approach. There is some strategy involved in this; you need to convince the host businesses to lend their endorsement and client contact list to you in exchange for something that will benefit them.

Introduce your product or service. Present your offering to the host business as though you were presenting to your potential clients: heavy on benefits, and light on features. Assume that the host business has placed themselves in the shoes of their clients, and is evaluating whether your product or service is worthwhile for them.

Provide marketing materials and other supporting information like testimonials and market research to establish your credibility, and your understanding of the people you are trying to reach.

Inform and excite. Provide as much information about how the HB Relationship will work, and be sincere in your efforts. Leave room for their thoughts and contributions to ensure that they buy into the process.

Get them excited about the opportunity you've placed in front of them. Use bright examples, and tell a hypothetical story about one of their clients benefiting from your service. Then, bring it back to the benefits that the relationship or partnership will deliver to their business.

Include an incentive. Be clear about the benefits the host can expect to receive. While you will not always be able to offer

Profits and Leads through Host-Beneficiary Relationships

something tangible, do your best to offer some incentive to the prospective host business.

If you are an established business, offer them reverse access to your client database after the initial mailing. Or, if it is allowable in your State, offer them a piece of the profits you receive from their clients. Whatever it is, make sure you articulate how this particular partnership is worth their while.

Communicate your rationale. Tell the host why you chose to approach them in particular. Do they enjoy a great reputation in the community? Are they a well-known business with a great sense of camaraderie? Compliment them on their business skills and the great relationships they have built with their clients and in the community.

Then, explain how your business can add value to theirs, and allow them to build on the existing relationships with their clients by offering your services.

Reassure. Communicate the benefits of the HB Relationship to the host, and reassure them that there is no risk involved for them. You are not out to take their profits, or place burden on their resources.

Remind them that you are seeking a complementary business relationship, one that benefits both parties.

Craft Your Message

Once you have secured your host partner, put the plan into action as quickly as possible. Offering to write the letter to their clients will not only give you control over the messaging of the offer, but also reduce the time investment required by the host. The process is simplified for them, and happens sooner for you.

- Just like sales letters and other marketing collateral, your HB offer letter should engage the reader and make them feel as though their needs and interests are cared for.
- The letter should position the host as a thoughtful service provider who sought out an offer specifically for the target audience.
- Your offer should be strong and slightly outrageous. Give a gift or something special, exclusively to this target audience.
- Remember to acknowledge the needs and troubles of your reader, and position your service as the answer or solution.

Five Simple Steps to Creating an HB Relationship

In summary, here are is a five-step roadmap to creating a positive, profit-filled, HB Relationship:

- Identify your target market.
- Identify target host businesses.
- Create a unique offer for each host business.
- Approach the host business.

Draft your letter.
Points to Remember

- **Make mistakes in small batches.** If you are unsure about the accuracy of your target market – do a test run. Send a small batch of 50-100 letters to a small group of people, and measure the response.

- o Alternately, you can send three different letters to each third of your target market, and evaluate which offer is acted on the most. This is of benefit for both the host and the beneficiary business because the response rate of the target market is tested, as are their purchase motivations.
- **Create benefit for the host business.** Remember that there must be an incentive for the host business, or the partnership is not worth the time investment. It is important to consider this, and plan ahead before you approach the host business. Create a number of options for the host to choose from, whether it is using your database after the initial mailing, or sharing a piece of the profits.
- **Be honest.** If you are working with several businesses in your area on different offers, make sure each business knows and is comfortable with the arrangement. Ensure that each offer is distinctive and each host is benefiting from the arrangement without competing with other host businesses. This is just good business form.
- **Rest on the strength of your offer.** With a strong offer, your HB campaign will be on the path to success. Make it something your audience can't refuse. Your offer should not only be enticing and engaging for your audience, but should also benefit the host in reputation. Their clients should feel

valued and appreciative toward the host for bringing your offer forward.

- **Repeat.** Once you've established one successful HB partnership, keep going! This technique is a valuable way to promote your business and your services, and can be repeated several times each year with several different host businesses.

Host Beneficiary Letter Template

[Headline in bold at the top of the page – strong statement or question] *[Optional sub headline to explain or answer the question/statement]*

Dear [name],

I hope this letter finds you well and enjoying your new home. Remember, your continued satisfaction with our [service] is guaranteed.

I am writing because I have stumbled upon an exclusive new [home, property, etc.] that will [describe how the property will meet a need or solve a problem].

[Beneficiary business name] is a [describe business type] that [describe business function]. I recently met with the owner, and was able to secure an unbelievable rate for my existing clients. The [product or service] is [describe product or service briefly]. Clients who have already purchased have said:

[list testimonials in bullet form]

Profits and Leads through Host-Beneficiary Relationships

[describe limited time or quantity], we are pleased to offer you [describe unique offer here]. This is an opportunity you will not find anywhere else, and an offer that will not be available in stores.

I hope you will be able to take advantage of this amazing [product or service].

Sincerely,

[your name]

[company name]

[phone number]

HB Relationship Worksheet

Target Market:	
Potential Host 1: Name: Business Type:	**Unique Offer:**
Host Benefits:	**Date Contacted:**
	☐ Accepted ☐ Follow-up
Notes:	

Target Market:	
Potential Host 2: Name: Business Type:	**Unique Offer:**
Host Benefits:	**Date Contacted:**
	☐ Accepted ☐ Follow-up
Notes:	

8

Use Press Releases for Instant Profit

Make Your Business News

The best kind of free advertising is an article in the newspaper, or a story on the radio, shining positive light on your business. Just like a testimonial, the printed words of a journalist are worth at least ten times more than the words in your advertising. Likewise, negative articles and reviews can cause just as much impact on your business – the kind of impact you don't want.

So how do you get your business news into the press? Better still, how do you make sure the press gets positive, accurate information about your business?

The simplest way to communicate with the media is through press releases. Press releases are a standard form of communication with the media, used to announce, communicate, and correct *newsworthy* information.

Press releases are not sales letters, or even newsletters. Their purpose is not to make a sale – although they may lead to sales – because they are not written for your client. Their purpose is to communicate news to the people that write the news, in a way that makes them take notice and care about what you have to say.

What are Effective Press Releases?

Effective press releases get your story covered. They hook editors on your angle, and encourage journalists to write about your news. They are concise, engaging, and written *with the media in mind*.

It's a good idea to sit down with your colleagues, family, and friends to test your story idea for newsworthiness. They'll be able to help you brainstorm angles and strategically plan your release.

Before you sit down to write your press release, ask yourself the following questions:

Is your story newsworthy?

If you're not used to writing press releases, spend some time thinking about this question. Of course your story is newsworthy to *you*, but why should other people care? Why does this story *matter* to the newspaper's readers? Newsworthy items are relevant, current, useful, and of importance to the community. They provide answers to the five "W's" (who, what, where, when and why).

Do you have an angle?

So your item is newsy, but what's the *angle*? Sure your company has had a record year for revenue, but what makes it unique? What makes your news an engaging story that is relevant to people outside your office? A press release should have at least one solid angle, or story idea, for the journalist. If the media have to spend time finding the story buried in your press release, you have an unlikely chance of getting covered.

Is now the right time to tell your story?

You may have a newsy story and an interesting angle, but is now the best time to tell your story? Be strategic about timing – for the benefit of your business, and for the likelihood of getting coverage. If you're a retailer featuring a new product line in October, is there benefit in waiting until November to announce your news, when consumers are shopping for the holidays? Did the newspaper you're targeting just run a big feature on the competition? Are you waiting on other potential news that you could announce at the same time?

Is your story true?

Reporting inaccurate or exaggerated facts is bad form, and can wreak havoc on your reputation. While you wouldn't do this intentionally, check to make sure you're not embellishing the facts to create a more interesting story. Journalists are always trying to dig out the real scoop, so if you feed them garbage, they'll smell it.

Who needs to know your story?

When you craft a press release, you need to be clear on who you want to read your story. Once you know exactly who your target audience is, you can narrow your focus down to the media that reach that audience. From there, you can cater your press release to the journalists who work for those outlets.

Writing Effective Press Releases

Here are some general rules and guidelines for crafting the perfect press release. Be prepared to write a few different versions, and make substantial edits; it takes a while to get it right. If writing is not your strongest skill, consider hiring a freelance writer to describe your news. Some online press release distribution services also offer writing services, so consider your options.

- **Craft a killer headline.** Just like advertisements, you have seconds to grab the media's attention with your headline. The headline should tell the story and answer the question *why does it matter?* Or, *why should I care?*

- **Spend time on the lead.** The lead is the first paragraph of your press release. It answers the five "W's" and provides enough detail to make the journalist or editor read on. Write a few different leads, each with a different story angle, and see which one has the most impact. If you haven't hooked them by now, consider your press release in the recycle bin.

- **Write for the newspaper.** Make your release easy to read, and easy for the journalist to work with. Occasionally, especially in communities with limited reporting resources, press releases are run with only some slight rewriting. In the best case, your release becomes the base for a feature article. Spend some time reading the publication you're targeting, and noticing the style in which it is written.

- **Notice newspaper style.** Generally, articles (and press releases) are written in an inverse pyramid format, where the

Use Press Releases for Instant Profit

most important information is as the top, and less important information follows in decreasing order of importance.

- **Use simple language.** Sentences written in simple style, with minimal description, embellishment, and flowery style are all that should appear in the release. Make sure each word has a purpose, and keep it tight. Only use the space you need to tell the story, no more.

- **Use examples to support your facts.** If you're sending a press release highlighting an achievement or accomplishment, prove it. Show the media that there are events and facts to back up your claims – cause and effect. This illustrates and tells a story, which is always more interesting and engaging than proud statements and quotes.

- **Skip industry jargon.** While industry phrases and terms may mean something to your colleagues and clients, they mean nothing to the media and the general public. Limit the amount of jargon you include in your release, and provide succinct explanations for uncommon terms you must use. Keep the language simple and easy to understand.

- **Use quotes sparingly.** Quotes are great ways to back up facts, add personality to your news, and include a new voice in the release. When writing quotes, keep them authentic, concise, and limited to two sources. Quotes from more than two sources in one release becomes cluttered and confusing.

- **Tell them who you are!** At the end of the release, be sure to include a short paragraph about your company that describes who you are, what you do, and a brief history.

- **Include as much contact information as possible.** Include one or two contact names, their titles, phone numbers, email addresses, website address and cell phone numbers. Make it as easy as possible for media to contact you.

Distribution

Media Target List

A database of local media is a key tool for any small business. Whether this list is used for an ad campaign, or media relations, it is important to know the players in your local media market.

Depending on your needs – and the size of your desired reach – there are a number of ways to create this list. If you are sticking to local and regional daily media, you and your employees can easily create and maintain your database.

If you're looking to have a broader reach, there are a number of online services that provide access to client media lists on a one-time or subscriber basis. These services typically have the most up to date information, as well as more detailed information about media contacts that you would not find on the internet.

This list should include the name of the publication, the type of publication, the publication's frequency, a contact name, phone number and email address. In most outlets, journalists are assigned to "beats" or subjects to cover, like business, crime, health, and community. If you know that you are targeting the business section of the newspaper, make sure your release ends up in the hands of the business editor or reporter. Just like your marketing materials, you need to make sure your message ends up in the right hands.

Draft Media List

Outlet	Type	Name	Email	Phone
Daily News	*Newspaper*	*Jill Smith*	*jsmith@dailynews.com*	*222.555.9878*

Email Distribution

The easiest and most common form of press release distribution is by email. However, journalists are bombarded by emails and it is easy for yours to get lost in the pile. Here are some tips to make sure it gets read, and not immediately deleted.

- **Don't send attachments.** Put your news release in text format in the body of the email with simple formatting to make sure it gets read. Attachments get stuck in junk mail filters, and emails from unknown sources with attachments get deleted.

- **Put the headline in the subject line.** Make sure you grab the attention of your recipient with the subject line to entice them to open the email. Don't assume that everything you send will be opened. Generic subject lines get buried in inboxes, or deleted.

- **Include a personal introduction or pitch.** While this can be time consuming, this is a nice strategy to implement when sending your release to your top ten media targets. Write a personal greeting before the release that hooks them on the story angle immediately. Keep it short, and if possible, include an acknowledgement of one of their recent stories that relates to your news.

Distribution Services

There are also a number of reputable press release distribution networks that will distribute your release to a broad audience. Sites like prnewswire.com allow you to send your release to state, province, country, or international market. These services

Use Press Releases for Instant Profit

also often provide writing or editing assistance, and can be valuable one-stop-shops.

Top 10 Press Release Mistakes

1. Errors in Grammar. Journalists are professional writers with a solid understanding of grammar and punctuation. Don't distract them from your news with spelling mistakes and poorly composed sentences. If writing isn't your strong suit, hire someone to write or proofread your release before you send it.

2. Too much content. The press release is intended to hook the editor, communicate the facts, and reek of newsworthiness. Once the editor or journalist is pursuing your story, you can provide them with more information and people to talk to. Stick to two pages double-spaced, max.

3. Too little content. You want to keep your release short and simple, but make sure you include all the necessary facts to support and illustrate the story. Make sure the five "W's" are answered, and all the correct contact information has been provided.

4. Not BCC'ing recipients. Before you send your release, double check that you haven't put all recipients in the "To" field of your email. Doing so announces who you're sending the information to, when all the recipients are competitors looking to break a story. Use the BCC field, and address the release to yourself.

5. Sending first thing Monday morning. A journalist's inbox is the most overloaded first thing in the morning – especially on Mondays. Typically, journalists will meet with editors in the morning to review editorial assignments, then work to a midafternoon deadline. The best time to call and email a reporter is mid-to-late afternoon, when their deadline has passed and their inbox has been sorted through.

6. Releases that read like ads. Your press release is not an advertisement, so don't write it like one. A journalist's job is to communicate pertinent, relevant, newsworthy information to their audience, not convince them to buy your product. Avoid overused advertising catch phrases like "limited time offer" and "this won't last long!" Your job here is to communicate, not to sell.

7. Not securing permission. Make sure you have permission to mention companies other than yours, to quote sources, and to submit images of your clients and employees to the press. Not having permission for these items can result in your story getting pulled at the last minute.

8. Sending to multiple editors at one outlet. Pick the editor who will be most interested in your news at each target news organization, and send your release to them only. This will avoid duplication of efforts at the outlet. Often, if an editor is not interested in your news, but knows an associate editor who will be, they will give you another contact name or pass the news on directly.

9. Sending to every outlet in town. The local motorbike magazine doesn't care about news from a baby clothing business. Make sure the media on your list are the media who would realistically cover your news. Sending information that does not align with the publication's subject matter will show you haven't done your research.

10. Following up the day you send the release. It may take a few days for an editor to respond to – or even read – your release. Be patient, and wait at least a week before following up. Even then, don't assume that your release has been read or remembered. Use the opportunity to pitch the editor over the phone on your story idea, or try a new angle.

Press Release Template

For Immediate Release Date

SMART, CATCHY HEADLINE IN BOLD, CAPITALS, CENTERED AT THE TOP OF THE PAGE
Sub headline, If Some Description is Required, In Title Case Beneath Headline

City, Province OR Neighborhood, City in italics – This is the "Lead" paragraph. This paragraph should include the pertinent information – *who, what, where, and why it matters to the editor's audience.* Put yourself in the editor or journalist's shoes – why should they cover this story? Why does it matter to their readers? Is it newsworthy?

The second paragraph should elaborate on the content from the lead paragraph, and usually includes a quote from a key person (principal, president, etc.) that communicates a feeling, belief, or general view of the issue.

The third paragraph is a brief history of the event, achievement or subject of the news release. How did the company get there? What did they do to achieve this? How long have they been working to get here?

The fourth paragraph can be another quote – share another perspective or a rationale behind any controversial issues. It can also elaborate or continue from the first quote.

The fifth paragraph is about the audience – how will they benefit? What does this mean to them? What are the next steps? *The audience can include a residential community, business community, industry, etc.*

The sixth paragraph can highlight key points in bullet format – deadlines, dates, milestones, report highlights, key features, event details, etc.

The last paragraphs are used to explain more about the company – what have they done that is related to this or newsworthy? Explain more about the process – how do you achieve this? Include any other pertinent information that the audience will need to know about next steps, what to watch for etc. Include more quotes from key sources.

Use Press Releases for Instant Profit

High resolution images of (xxx) are available upon request

Ends. *This shows to the reader that the news release is over.*

Media Contact *no more than two contacts, these people must be available as soon as the release is sent out*

Name, Position
Organization
Phone
Email

Press Release Sample – New Product

For Immediate Release
August 23, 2010

MOMS ON WHEELS TO DELIVER NUTRITIOUS MEALS AT SCHOOL THIS SEPTEMBER
New lunchtime service to provide kids with balanced snacks and meals

Cartwright, California – Attention busy moms: scratch lunches of your list. Moms on Wheels is expanding this September, providing daily lunch service for elementary school students with busy families. Parents can now subscribe to daily or weekly deliveries, and trust that convenient, healthy bag lunches are arriving at their children's classroom.

"As a mother, one of my biggest challenges is making sure my two sons go to school with a healthy and balanced lunch," says Moms on Wheels co-founder and dietician Barbara Jones. "Between grocery shopping, preparing meals, packing lunch, and making sure it winds up in their backpacks, it was taking up a lot of my time."

Use Press Releases for Instant Profit

Moms on Wheels prepares lunches fresh every morning, then delivers to 20 elementary schools by 12:30pm. Lunch menus vary from wraps and sandwiches, to cheese and crackers, with an assortment of seasonal vegetables, fruit and a cookie.

Moms on Wheels offers daily and weekly meal options, and caters to dietary and allergy requirements. Starting at just $3 a day, the service is affordable for every family and can be customized to a specific budget. Family rates are also available for parents with multiple children in school.

The innovative service is the brainchild of Barbara Jones and Lindsay Lee who established the meal service last year to deliver lunches once a week to local elementary schools. Jones and Lee plan to expand the service to hot items next year, when they move to an expanded kitchen facility.

To register, contact Moms on Wheels at 555.325.9872 or www.healthylunchesforkids.com. All elementary students will be bringing home an information form during the first week of school this year.

Ends.

Media Contact

A Profit Manual for Realtors®

Barbara Jones, Co-Founder

Moms on Wheels

555.325.9872

bjones@healthylunchesforkids.com

Press Release Sample – Accomplishment

For Immediate Release
November 12, 2009

CARR'S CARPET CLEANING SWEEPS UP WITH BUSINESS OF THE YEAR AWARD

Local business wins four accolades at annual Chamber of Commerce event

Bend, Oregon – You could say that Carr's Carpet Cleaning Services truly 'cleaned up' this year; the local business was honored with an award in four categories at the annual Chamber of Commerce Business Awards. Carr's Carpet Cleaning earned Employer of the Year Award, Story of the Year Award, Fastest Growing Business, and the prestigious Business of the Year Award.

"We are thrilled and amazed at the generous recognition we received as a company last night," said owner Jerry Owens. "These awards were earned by every member of our staff, and the terrific job they do servicing our clients."

Carr's Carpet Cleaning was established by local Bend resident Jerry Owens just three years ago at the age of 22. Starting out with a small business loan from his grandfather, Gerald Carr,

Owens has built the company into a thriving business of 25 employees, serving five communities in the region. This year, Owens introduced three new services: furniture cleaning, duct cleaning, and stain protection treatment.

"It is always such a challenge to decide on a single recipient in each of the award categories, especially since there are so many reputable businesses in our community that deserve recognition," says Peter Smith, President of the Bend Chamber of Commerce. "However, we were very impressed with Mr. Owen's story, and the incredible growth of Carr's Carpet Cleaning over the last year."

Carr's Carpet Cleaning provides regular cleaning services to clients across the region, and offers free custom quotations, and a full satisfaction, money-back guarantee. Carr's uses a premium steam method for stain removal that eliminates marks and odors in a single treatment. With two brand new cleaning units, Carr's also now offers complete stain prevention treatments – an ideal worry-free service for families with young children.

The Chamber of Commerce Business Awards are held annually to recognize business achievement in the Bend area. For a complete list of award recipients, please contact the Chamber directly at 555.333.7659. Deadline for nominations for next year's awards is August 31, 2010.

High resolution images of the awards presentations are available upon request

Ends.

Media Contacts:

Jerry Owens	Peter Smith
Carr's Carpet Cleaning	*Chamber of Commerce*
555.333.4337	555.333.9870
jowens@carrscarpets.com	
psmith@brooksown.com	

A Profit Manual for Realtors®

Press Release Sample – Controversy

Note: When faced with a controversy that may affect the reputation of your business, consider hiring professional public relations counsel. These professionals are trained to handle challenging media relations scenarios, and can help to determine the best strategy for information disclosure.

For Immediate Release
December 15, 2009

HOLIDAY SPRUCE OFFERS FREE CHRISTMAS TREE REPLACEMENT TO ALL RESIDENTS
Trees sprayed with dangerous chemical to be removed and replaced at no charge

Halifax, Nova Scotia – Holiday Spruce announced today that 75 per cent of the Christmas Trees for sale at their Bend Street farm have been mistreated with a chemical component that may be dangerous if repeatedly inhaled or accidentally ingested. The Christmas tree farm is offering free removal and replacements for all families affected.

"We at Holiday Spruce are appalled by the circumstances that allowed our clients and families to take home mistreated

Use Press Releases for Instant Profit

Christmas trees," says Spruce Manager Tim Smith. "We sincerely apologize to the families affected by these events, and are committed to removing and replacing every single tree within the next four days."

Holiday Spruce is currently investigating the cause of the chemical mistreatment, and has closed their Bend Street farm for the season. All clients who have purchased their holiday trees at Spruce are asked to contact their replacement line at 555.342.9020.

"We have maintained a record of each purchase made this year, and are currently in the process of contacting clients and arranging for immediate removal," says Smith. "Holiday Spruce will be purchasing trees from our associates, and delivering them to clients within the next four days."

Holiday Spruce is a seasonal tree farm on Bend Road that has been in operation for nearly 15 years. A family favorite for Christmas tree purchases, the farm offers school group tours, hot apple cider, hot dogs, and roasted chestnuts.

Ends.

Media Contact:

Tim Smith, Manager
Holiday Spruce
t. 555.342.9087
c. 555.768.3422
tsmith@holidaysprucetrees.com

9

Profit from Direct Mail

Every time you mail an existing or potential client a letter and ask them to respond or take action, you are running a direct-mail campaign.

Direct mail is a marketing strategy that can help you achieve a number of business objectives. From lead generation to client retention, direct mail campaigns are a highly versatile and relatively cost-effective choice for business promotion.

What you probably don't realize is that direct mail is one of the most targeted marketing strategies you can implement, and one of the easiest to track, measure and analyze results.

It is also one of the most personal. Instead of an advertisement, flyer, newspaper insert or catalogue, you are sending each client a personalized letter that is tailored to their unique needs and desires.

Getting the most out of your direct mail campaign is easy. With a laser-sharp mailing list and irresistible offer, your direct mail campaign can easily flood your business with qualified leads.

Let's get started!

A List of Ideal Clients

Unless you spend time carefully crafting a mailing list of ideal clients, you may as well pack and up go home. The success of a direct mail campaign largely rests on the pinpoint accuracy of your mailing list.

The only people you want on your list are your potential "ideal clients." The people who are most likely to buy or list a property with you, and who are a delight to deal with. They are the type of people who will account for 80% of your revenue, and just 20% of your total client base.

You have a number of options when you are creating your mailing list:

- **Existing client database**. This is a list of all of the people who have previously bought or listed with you. It is important to gather their full contact information at the time of sale so you will be able to get contact them again.

- **Existing leads database**. This is a list of all of the leads that have come through your door, but have not done business with you. This may include those who responded to your last direct mail campaign, but have not yet become clients.

- **Outsourced list**. This is a list that has been purchased from a market research firm, the government, or the post office. These lists are pulled based on demographic information – age, sex, location, income, family structure, etc.

Putting the mailing list together

Once you have determined the source(s) for your mailing list, you will have to spend some time assembling it and preparing it for your mailing.

1. Make sure all contacts are up to date. Phone old contacts to confirm their mailing address. An out-of-date list will cost you money in printing and postage.

2. Ensure all contacts are accurate to the list criteria. Take a read through your list to make sure there are no contacts that shouldn't be on the list.

3. Use a database management program to manage your mailing. This will allow you to keep a master list, and create custom lists for each mailing. Remember to save the file name as something that describes the mailing so you can easily find it.

Writing Effective Direct Mail Pieces

Now that you have a laser-sharp mailing list, you will want to do everything you can to target your message to the recipients on your list.

An effective direct mail piece:

- **Has a clear structure.** The piece is clearly a letter – there is an engaging headline, clear message, point form list of benefits, and postscript.
- **Features an irresistible offer.** The purchase opportunity is too good for the target audience to refuse. It includes an element of scarcity and urgency.
- **Focuses on client benefits.** The client clearly understands

"what's in it for me?" The product or service is clearly positioned as something of value and a solution to a need, problem, or desire.

- **Is personal and conversational.** The letter is personally addressed, and reads as though it was composed specifically for the recipient. It is written in conversational tone, with short sentences and limited description.
- **Is short.** The letter communicates what it needs to, and closes. It does not go on for pages in length. The messages are clear, succinct, and simple.
- **Is urgent.** The piece gives the reader to act immediately. There is a time limit or a quantity limit to the offer that requires an urgent response.
- **Includes a Postscript.** The offer or urgency is repeated after the signature at the bottom of the letter. Like a headline, everyone will read the P.S.

The Five-Step Direct Mail Campaign

1. Determine Your Target Audience

As we discussed above, you will want to ensure that you have the most accurate, targeted list possible for your direct mail campaign.

Be clear about the purpose for your direct mail campaign – this will help you decide if you want to send your letters to your entire target market, a segment of that market, existing clients, or potentially a referring business's clients. Then you can determine how you craft your offer, how you structure your letter, and when

Profit from Direct Mail

you choose to send it.

2. Choose what you want to say

What is the message you want to communicate to your target list? What can you offer them that will entice them to act immediately?

Create a specific offer for each direct mail campaign to ensure each time you communicate with your target list you have something new to say. Tailor this offer to each mailing list.

Decide what product or service benefits will be most compelling to your target audience, and include those benefits prominently in your letter.

3. Develop a compelling direct mail piece

You are in control of how your format your message. Are you sending a letter? A brochure and a letter? A postcard? The format of your direct mail piece needs to be tailored to your target list, and reflect your product or service. A younger audience may respond to a postcard, but an older audience may appreciate a formalized letter.

Ensure that whatever format you choose, the piece is professionally designed, prominently includes your logo and company branding, and is professionally produced.

This piece of paper has to act as an ambassador of your company – you absolutely need it to appear impressive and professional.

4. Pick your timing

Some products and purchase decisions are best made at certain times of the year, or the month. Consider the best purchase windows for the people in your target marketing. When are they most likely to consider moving?

Anticipate these windows, and time your direct mail campaign accordingly.

5. Follow up

Comprehensive follow up to a direct mail campaign means two things:

1. Following up on your letter with a phone call or second letter

Often it takes more than a letter to get a potential client to take action. This can be a result of the accuracy of your mailing list, your offer, the time of the year, or the quality of the marketing material (brochure). If you are certain that your mailing list is accurate and up to date, follow up with a phone call, or send another letter.

2. Recording, measuring and analyzing your results.

It is essential that you evaluate each direct mail campaign based on your time and financial investment and your rate of response. How else will you be able to tell if it was a successful or effective strategy?

For each campaign, record and analyze the following information:

- Number of letters sent
- Number or responses as a percentage
- Number of sales directly resulting from the campaign
- Number of enquiries
- Total value of sales directly resulting from the campaign

Based on this information, determine if the campaign was successful (did it make you money?) or not. Consider making some changes to your list, your offer, or the piece itself, and try again.

10

Organize Your Office for Success

Have you ever tried to cook a fancy gourmet dinner in a messy kitchen?

It starts out okay. I have all the ingredients I need; it just takes me a little longer to find them as I go. I have to find and clear some counter space, then wipe the crumbs off of it and grab a knife.

Some pots are clean, so I use them first. But then I need the double boiler, and it's still crusted with last night's meal, so I have to wash it. While I'm washing the pot, the garlic and onion that I'm sautéing starts to burn, so I have to run over and rescue it.

Pretty soon, I'm running around like crazy, trying to rescue each item I cook because I'm busy preparing what I need for the next dish. It should be no surprise that the meal was a disaster.

Your place of work is just like your kitchen. It needs to be clean, well-organized, and ready to function. Your tools need to be prepared and at the ready in order to support the tasks you and your staff need to complete.

A well set-up office – with all the necessary tools – will save you time and the expense of redundancy. This is the first key to an effective and successful business operation.

Create an Office for Profitability

Most people understand the relationship between time management and profitability. Effective time management increases productivity; more work can be completed in less time, with less distraction and waste.

Office organization also affects profitability and productivity. A tidy and well-structured office is not only a more pleasant place to work, but it also reduces the time anyone might spend looking for items and digging through loose paperwork.

A well-organized office also encourages better internal communication. There are clear areas of the business that are designated for sales news, target tracking, and project planning. This fosters team building and collaborative work ethic.

Getting Started: Workspace Audit

The best place to start is by taking an honest inventory of the current state of your office or working environment. With that information, you can determine what areas need to be improved, streamlined, or de-cluttered. Spend some time taking a look around your office and note the following:

- Is there a location where internal company information is displayed?
- What is the distance between your office and the printer or photocopier?
- How much loose paper is found around the business?
- What is hung up on the walls?

Organize Your Office for Success

- Do your staff members have organization systems for their own desks?
- What can be found on your desk?
- How many files are used on a daily or weekly basis?
- Where are old or outdated files kept?

Organize Your Desk

Presumably, your desk is where you spend the most time in your office. It is where you are expected to be the most productive. To get all your important tasks completed.

Simply put, you will be more productive and effective if your workspace is clean and organized. Spend some time each day tidying and organizing your workspace – ideally when you are planning your work or your schedule for the following day.

Here are some other ways you can keep your immediate workspace in the most productive form possible:

Phone. Put your phone on the left side of the desk if you are right handed and on the right side of the desk if you are left handed. Keep a notebook by the phone to record messages and conversation notes. Also record phone messages here, and delete them from your system.

Personal Items. Keep person items out of your immediate line of sight. Pictures can be distracting, and points for daydreaming.

Organizer. Keep your Daytimer or appointment calendar easily accessible on your desk. Use this as your main system for notes, tasks, follow-up, and brainstorming. Keep the rest of your desk clear.

Files. Only keep the files you need on your desk. Store files you don't use daily or weekly in a filing cabinet further away.

Inbox and action items. Sort items in your inbox into an easily accessible file sorter or a stack of paper trays. Separate paper into the following categories: to-do, to-review, waiting response, on-hold, to file.

Organize Your Office

Take the information you gathered in your workplace audit and identify opportunities for improvement. Can the office benefit from a better layout? A paper management system? More clearly defined areas? A new filing system?

The answer will depend on the unique needs of your business, and take into account how you and your staff use the space. Here are some suggestions and guidelines for improving the organization of your office or place of business:

Establish Clear Areas

Divide your office into areas of productivity, and locate all related materials and equipment in each area.

Here are some sample areas you may wish to consider:

- Printing and photocopying
- Office supplies
- Financial paperwork and accounting
- Team gathering
- Kitchen or food-related preparation
- Reception
- Point of sale

Create a Central Location for Information

Many people – including your employees – learn and interpret information that is visual better than any other means of communication. A central location in your office for staff to go for company information and updates is an essential tool for team building and internal communications.

Every office needs:

Whiteboard

Place a whiteboard in an easily accessed place – your staff communication center or the boardroom. This whiteboard is for brainstorming, project planning, marketing planning, or any other use that may be required.

This is a great tool for team meetings, client meetings, and management meetings. The facilitator can diagram information and work through issues on the spot.

Sales Board

Create a customized sales board for your business. Take a whiteboard, and some thin black tape, and create a chart or diagram that records regular sales statistics and targets.

You may wish to separate the whiteboard into two sections – target sales and actual sales, and compare based on weekly, quarterly, and yearly targets. You can also compare actual sales to sale for the same period the previous year.

A Profit Manual for Realtors®

12-Month Marketing Planner

Chart your marketing plan on a large calendar and post it in a central area. This is a clear reminder of the big picture, and each of the promotions you have planned over the course of the year.

Remember to write in dry-erase marker so you can easily make changes. Consider color-coding your promotions or projects for easy visibility.

Manage Paper + Filing

System	Steps
Create a master filing system and color code it	Group vendor files (accounts payable) and assign a color Group client files (accounts receivable) and assign a color Group project or product files and assign a color
Sort each filing category by date or alphabetically by name	Sort vendor or supplier files by name Sort client files by client number or name Sort project files by project number or name
Create a binder of master lists for regularly accessed information	Office passwords Financial accounts Goals Birthdays Vendor contact information
Use a bound notebook	Keep track of phone calls and messages Put the date on each page Eliminate loose notepaper

Organize Your Office for Success

Get rid of magazines and other reading material	Throw away industry magazines and newspapers Keep relevant articles of interest Sort them into files, if necessary
Keep tax-related documents in one spot	File all receipts, donations and other tax related information in the same filing cabinet Make copies of documents you need to file in more than one spot
Create a business care management system	Throw away old business cards Organize cards by last name or company name in a binder or rolodex Enter the information in a data management program, then throw away the cards

So What Do You Do From Here?

Take action! If you are already an accomplished business owner burning in excess of $200,000 per year, use this book as direction to enhance the speed of your business success.

The amazing thing about the game of marketing and sales is that when you put proven processes to work and continue to follow them, and abundance of success will follow. The biggest mistake is to start a process and then fall back into your old habits after a short time. thing to do is:

A) Read this book

B) Implement the strategies in this book

C) Call Vince for periodic review and modification to your Marketing & Sales strategies.

Concentrate on strategies to learn and the turn will follow! If you are serious about taking the next step then go to work on yourself, study other Realtor's® successes, understand marketing strategies and become a sponge for new material. The amazing thing about the game of marketing and sales is that when you put proven processes to work and continue to follow them, and abundance of and success will follow. The biggest mistake is to start a process and then fall back into your old habits after a short time.

Above all, get the knowledge you need to before you step onto the field. Think about it, if you were going to challenge Michael Jordan to a game of basketball for money, wouldn't it make sense to learn the game and practice before you stepped onto the court? It is amazing to me how many new brokers and individual Realtors® start the game of business against seasoned professionals, the competition, without the first developing the necessary knowledge to be successful. Then they feel and blame the market, the economy, their location, the clients, etc.

If you have not yet managed to create wealth and systems that allow you to take time off, fill retirement accounts or pay for your children's college, then learn and master the steps outlined in my book. I am a huge advocate of education and mentorships. Get the right information, find someone that knows how to walk you through them and watch your quality of life take new shape.

To learn how to avoid the three key mistakes all small and medium firms make, visit

www.EliteMarketingAndSalesCoach.com

www.ingramcontent.com/pod-product-compliance
Lightning Source LLC
Chambersburg PA
CBHW052323220526
45472CB00001B/251